W9-AHD-391

ANIMAL CLASSES

Fish

by Kari Schuetz

BELLWETHER MEDIA · MINNEAPOLIS, MN

Note to Librarians, Teachers, and Parents:

Blastoff! Readers are carefully developed by literacy experts and combine standards-based content with developmentally appropriate text.

Level 1 provides the most support through repetition of high-frequency words, light text, predictable sentence patterns, and strong visual support.

Level 2 offers early readers a bit more challenge through varied simple sentences, increased text load, and less repetition of high-frequency words.

Level 3 advances early-fluent readers toward fluency through increased text and concept load, less reliance on visuals, longer sentences, and more literary language.

Level 4 builds reading stamina by providing more text per page, increased use of punctuation, greater variation in sentence patterns, and increasingly challenging vocabulary.

Level 5 encourages children to move from "learning to read" to "reading to learn" by providing even more text, varied writing styles, and less familiar topics.

Whichever book is right for your reader, Blastoff! Readers are the perfect books to build confidence and encourage a love of reading that will last a lifetime!

This edition first published in 2013 by Bellwether Media, Inc.

No part of this publication may be reproduced in whole or in part without written permission of the publisher. For information regarding permission, write to Bellwether Media, Inc., Attention: Permissions Department, 5357 Penn Avenue South, Minneapolis, MN 55419.

Library of Congress Cataloging-in-Publication Data
Schuetz, Kari.
Fish / by Kari Schuetz.
p. cm. – (Blastoff! readers: animal classes)
Includes bibliographical references and index.
Summary: "Simple text and full-color photography introduce beginning readers to fish. Developed by literacy experts for students in kindergarten through third grade"–Provided by publisher.
ISBN 978-1-60014-773-9 (hardcover : alk. paper)
1. Fishes–Juvenile literature. I. Title.
QL617.2S37 2013
597–dc23 2011053035

Text copyright © 2013 by Bellwether Media, Inc. BLASTOFF! READERS and associated logos are trademarks and/or registered trademarks of Bellwether Media, Inc. SCHOLASTIC, CHILDREN'S PRESS, and associated logos are

Table of Contents

The Animal Kingdom

All animals that live on land and under the sea are part of the animal kingdom.

They have many differences, but they fit into groups based on what they have in common.

What Are Fish?

Animals with backbones are called **vertebrates**. The fish **class** includes more than half of all vertebrates in the world. There are almost 30,000 known **species** of fish.

The Animal Kingdom

vertebrates

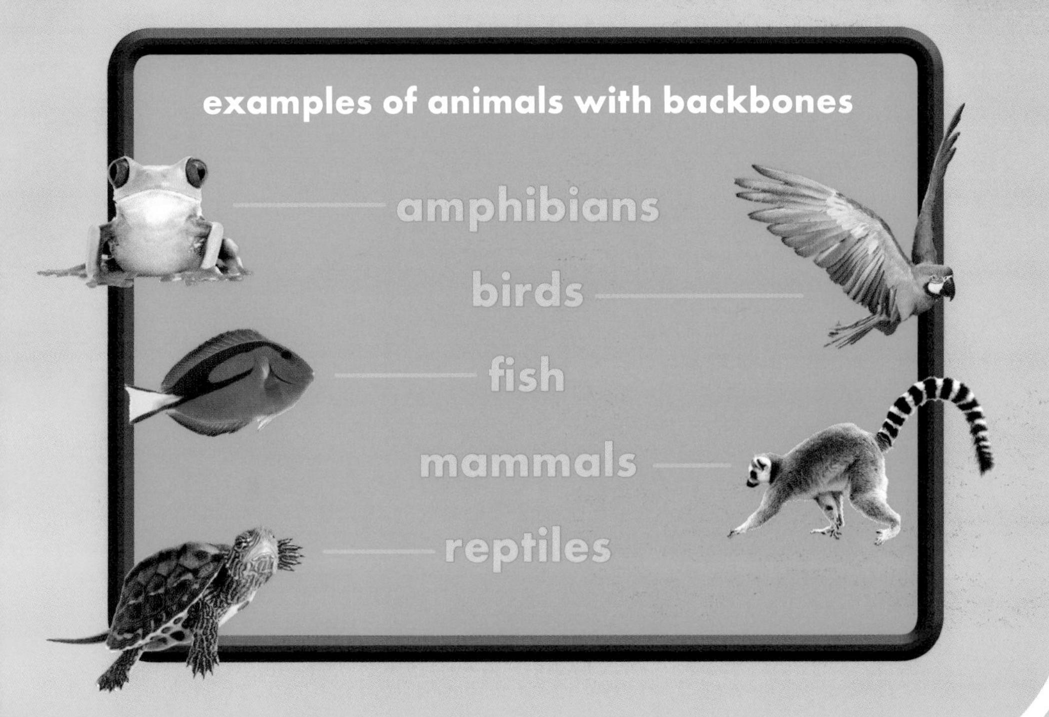

invertebrates

examples of animals without backbones

- arachnids
- crustaceans
- insects

Fish live **aquatic** lives. They swim in **freshwater**, **saltwater**, or both.

Fish are **cold-blooded** animals. This means their bodies are the same temperature as the water around them.

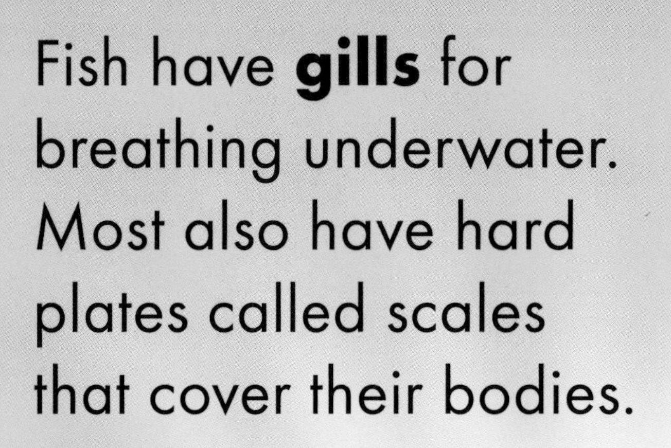

Fish have **gills** for breathing underwater. Most also have hard plates called scales that cover their bodies.

A layer of slime protects the scales of most fish. It also helps them move through water with ease.

gills

Fish use their **fins** to swim. The tail fin pushes a fish forward while the other fins steer.

tail fin

fins

Groups of Fish

lamprey

All fish belong to
one of three groups.
Hagfish and lampreys
form one group.

These are jawless
fish that look like
snakes without scales.
Their mouths are like
suction cups.

hagfish

Sharks, skates, and rays are another group. They have skeletons made of **cartilage** instead of bone.

Many members of this group can be dangerous. Sharks have razor-sharp teeth. Some rays sting or produce an electric shock!

shark

Bony fish are the largest group of fish. They have skeletons that are made of bone.

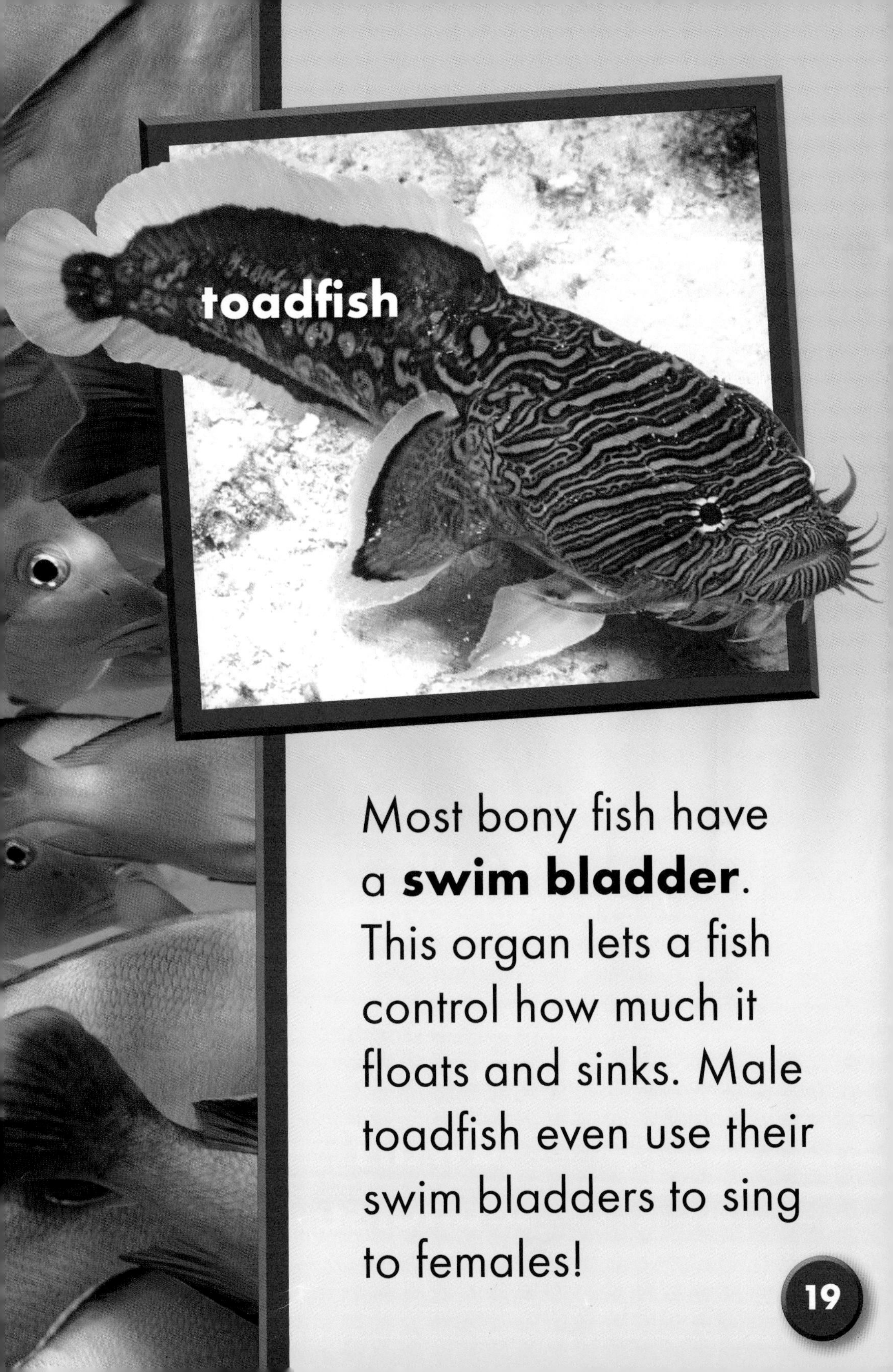

Most bony fish have a **swim bladder**. This organ lets a fish control how much it floats and sinks. Male toadfish even use their swim bladders to sing to females!

Fantastic Fish

Largest:
whale shark

Smallest:
paedocypris

Fastest:
sailfish

Slowest:
dwarf seahorse

Longest Life Span:
rougheye rockfish

Shortest Life Span:
seven-figure pygmy goby

dwarf seahorse

sailfish

Glossary

aquatic—living in water

cartilage—a strong, bendable material; some fish have skeletons made of cartilage.

class—a group within the animal kingdom; members of a specific class share many of the same characteristics.

cold-blooded—having a body temperature that changes to match the temperature of its surroundings

fins—body parts that fish use to swim through water

freshwater—water that is not salty; lakes and rivers contain freshwater.

gills—organs that allow fish to breathe underwater

saltwater—water that contains salt; oceans and seas are bodies of saltwater.

species—groups of related animals; all animals of a specific species have the same characteristics.

swim bladder—the organ that helps bony fish float or sink

vertebrates—members of the animal kingdom that have backbones

To Learn More

AT THE LIBRARY

Goldish, Meish. *Disgusting Hagfish.* New York, N.Y.: Bearport Pub., 2009.

Musgrave, Ruth. *National Geographic Kids Everything Sharks.* Washington, D.C.: National Geographic, 2011.

Swinney, Geoff. *Fish Facts.* Gretna, La.: Pelican Pub. Co., 2011.

ON THE WEB

Learning more about fish is as easy as 1, 2, 3.

1. Go to www.factsurfer.com.
2. Enter "fish" into the search box.
3. Click the "Surf" button and you will see a list of related Web sites.

With factsurfer.com, finding more information is just a click away.

Index